MARY

MARY

Grace and Hope in Christ

The Anglican-Roman Catholic International Commission
An agreed statement

HARRISBURG • LONDON

Morehouse Publishing, P.O. Box 1321, Harrisburg, PA 17105

Morehouse Publishing, The Tower Building, 11 York Road, London SE1 7NX

Morehouse Publishing is a Continuum imprint.

Published by Morehouse for the Anglican Consultative Council, London, and the Pontifical Council for Promoting Christian Unity, Rome

Unless otherwise indicated, biblical quotations are from the New Revised Standard Version Bible, copyright 1989, Division of Christian Education of the National Council of the Churches of Christ in the United States of America. Used by permission. All rights reserved.

Cover art: Basilica Di S Maria Sopra Minerva, Rome
Camera di St. Caterina da Siena
The Annunciation
Photo: PP Domenicani
By the kind courtesy of the branch of the department for Monuments and Artistic Treasures, Italy

Back cover art: Mary and Child
Anglican Church of St. Gregory and St. Martin, Wye, Kent, UK
Photo: Jim Rosenthal, Anglican Episcopal World

Cover design: Lee Singer

Library of Congress Cataloging-in-Publication Data

Anglican/Roman Catholic International Commission.
  Mary : grace and hope in Christ / the Anglican-Roman Catholic International Commission.
    p. cm.
  "An agreed statement."
  ISBN 0-8192-8132-8 (pbk.)
  1. Mary, Blessed Virgin, Saint. 2. Catholic Church--Doctrines. 3. Anglican Communion--Doctrines. 4. Catholic Church--Relations--Anglican Communion. 5. Anglican Communion--Relations--Catholic Church. I. Title.
  BT603.A54 2005
  232.91--dc22
                                    2005006385

Printed in the United Kingdom at MPG Books, Bodmin

05 06 07 08 09 10   10 9 8 7 6 5 4 3 2 1

✤
Contents

Preface by the Co-Chairmen

In the continuing journey toward full communion, the Roman Catholic Church and the Churches of the Anglican Communion have for many years prayerfully considered a number of questions concerning the faith we share and the way we articulate it in the life and worship of our two households of faith. We have submitted Agreed Statements to the Holy See and to the Anglican Communion for comment, further clarification if necessary, and conjoint acceptance as congruent with the faith of Anglicans and Roman Catholics.

In framing this Agreed Statement, we have drawn on the Scriptures and the common tradition which predates the Reformation and the Counter Reformation. As in previous Anglican-Roman Catholic International

Commission (ARCIC) documents, we have attempted to use language that reflects what we hold in common and transcends the controversies of the past. At the same time, in this statement we have had to face squarely dogmatic definitions which are integral to the faith of Roman Catholics but largely foreign to the faith of Anglicans. The members of ARCIC, over time, have sought to embrace one another's ways of doing theology and have considered together the historical context in which certain doctrines developed. In so doing, we have learned to receive anew our own traditions, illumined and deepened by the understanding of and appreciation for each other's tradition.

Our Agreed Statement concerning the Blessed Virgin Mary as pattern of grace and hope is a powerful reflection of our efforts to seek out what we hold in common and celebrates important aspects of our common heritage. Mary, the mother of our Lord Jesus Christ, stands before us as an exemplar of faithful obedience, and her "Be it to me according to your word" is the grace-filled response each of us is called to make to God, both personally and communally, as the Church, the body of Christ. It is as figure of the Church, her arms uplifted in prayer and praise, her hands open in receptivity and availability to the outpouring of the Holy Spirit, that we are one with Mary as she magnifies the Lord. "Surely," Mary declares in her song recorded in the Gospel of Luke, "from this day all generations will call me blessed."

Our two traditions share many of the same feasts associated with Mary. From our experience we have found that it is in the realm of worship that we realize our deepest convergence as we give thanks to God for the Mother of the Lord who is one with us in that vast community of love and prayer we call the communion of saints.

✠ Alexander J. Brunett

✠ Peter F. Carnley

Seattle

Feast of the Presentation

February 2, 2004

❖
The Status of
the Document

The document published here is the work of the Anglican–Roman Catholic International Commission (ARCIC). It is a joint statement of the Commission. The authorities who appointed the Commission have allowed the statement to be published so that it may be widely discussed. It is not an authoritative declaration by the Roman Catholic Church or by the Anglican Communion, who will study and evaluate the document in due course.

Citations from Scripture are normally taken from the New Revised Standard Version. In some cases the Commission has offered its own translation.

Mary: Grace and Hope in Christ

The Seattle Statement

INTRODUCTION

1 In honouring Mary as Mother of the Lord, all generations of Anglicans and Roman Catholics have
echoed the greeting of Elizabeth: "Blessed are you
among women, and blessed is the fruit of your
womb" (Luke 1:42). The Anglican–Roman Catholic
International Commission now offers this Agreed
Statement on the place of Mary in the life and doctrine of the Church in the hope that it expresses our
common faith about the one who, of all believers, is
closest to our Lord and Saviour Jesus Christ. We do
so at the request of our two Communions, in response
to questions set before us. A special consultation of

Anglican and Roman Catholic bishops, meeting under the leadership of the Archbishop of Canterbury, Dr George Carey, and Cardinal Edward I Cassidy, President of the Pontifical Council for Promoting Christian Unity at Mississauga, Canada, in 2000, specifically asked ARCIC for "a study of Mary in the life and doctrine of the Church." This request recalls the observation of the Malta Report (1968) that "real or apparent differences between us come to the surface in such matters as . . . the Mariological definitions" promulgated in 1854 and 1950. More recently, in *Ut Unum Sint* (1995), Pope John Paul II identified as one area in need of fuller study by all Christian traditions before a true consensus of faith can be achieved "the Virgin Mary, as Mother of God and Icon of the Church, the spiritual Mother who intercedes for Christ's disciples and for all humanity" (para. 79).

2 ARCIC has addressed this topic once before. *Authority in the Church II* (1981) already records a significant degree of agreement:

> We agree that there can be but one mediator between God and man, Jesus Christ, and reject any interpretation of the role of Mary which

obscures this affirmation. We agree in recognising that Christian understanding of Mary is inseparably linked with the doctrines of Christ and the Church. We agree in recognising the grace and unique vocation of Mary, Mother of God Incarnate (*Theotókos*), in observing her festivals, and in according her honour in the communion of saints. We agree that she was prepared by divine grace to be the mother of our Redeemer, by whom she herself was redeemed and received into glory. We further agree in recognising in Mary a model of holiness, obedience, and faith for all Christians. We accept that it is possible to regard her as a prophetic figure of the Church of God before as well as after the Incarnation. (para. 30)

The same document, however, points out remaining differences:

The dogmas of the Immaculate Conception and the Assumption raise a special problem for those Anglicans who do not consider that the precise definitions given by these dogmas are sufficiently supported by Scripture. For many Anglicans the teaching authority of the bishop

of Rome, independent of a council, is not rec-
ommended by the fact that through it these
Marian doctrines were proclaimed as dogmas
binding on all the faithful. Anglicans would also
ask whether, in any future union between our
two Churches, they would be required to sub-
scribe to such dogmatic statements. (para. 30)

These reservations in particular were noted in the
official *Response of the Holy See to The Final Report*
(1991, para. 13). Having taken these shared beliefs
and these questions as the starting point for our
reflection, we are now able to affirm further significant agreement on the place of Mary in the life and
doctrine of the Church.

3 The present document proposes a fuller statement of
our shared belief concerning the Blessed Virgin
Mary and so provides the context for a common
appreciation of the content of the Marian dogmas.
We also take up differences of practice, including the
explicit invocation of Mary. This new study of Mary
has benefited from our previous study of reception in
The Gift of Authority (1999). There we concluded that,
when the Church receives and acknowledges what it
recognizes as a true expression of the Tradition once

for all delivered to the Apostles, this reception is an act both of faithfulness and of freedom. The freedom to respond in fresh ways in the face of new challenges is what enables the Church to be faithful to the Tradition which it carries forward. At other times, some element of the apostolic Tradition may be forgotten, neglected, or abused. In such situations, fresh recourse to Scripture and Tradition recalls God's revelation in Christ: we call this process *re-reception* (cf. *Gift* 24–25). Progress in ecumenical dialogue and understanding suggests that we now have an opportunity to re-receive together the tradition of Mary's place in God's revelation.

4   Since its inception ARCIC has sought to get behind opposed or entrenched positions to discover and develop our common inheritance of faith (cf. *Authority I* 25). Following *The Common Declaration* in 1966 of Pope Paul VI and the Archbishop of Canterbury, Dr Michael Ramsey, we have continued our "serious dialogue . . . founded on the Gospels and on the ancient common traditions." We have asked to what extent doctrine or devotion concerning Mary belongs to a legitimate 'reception' of the apostolic Tradition, in accordance with the Scriptures. This Tradition has at its core the proclamation of the

trinitarian 'economy of salvation', grounding the life and faith of the Church in the divine communion of Father, Son, and Spirit. We have sought to understand Mary's person and role in the history of salvation and the life of the Church in the light of a theology of divine grace and hope. Such a theology is deeply rooted in the enduring experience of Christian worship and devotion.

5 God's grace calls for and enables human response (cf. *Salvation and the Church* [1987] 9). This is seen in the Gospel account of the Annunciation, where the angel's message evokes the response of Mary. The Incarnation and all that it entailed, including the passion, death, and resurrection of Christ and the birth of the Church, came about by way of Mary's freely uttered *fiat*—"let it be done to me according to your word" (Luke 1:38). We recognize in the event of the Incarnation God's gracious 'Yes' to humanity as a whole. This reminds us once more of the Apostle's words in 2 Corinthians 1:18–20 (*Gift* 8ff): all God's promises find their 'Yes' in the Son of God, Jesus Christ. In this context, Mary's *fiat* can be seen as the supreme instance of a believer's 'Amen' in response to the 'Yes' of God. Christian disciples respond to the same 'Yes' with their own 'Amen'. They thus know themselves to be children together of the one heav-

enly Father, born of the Spirit as brothers and sisters of Jesus Christ, drawn into the communion of love of the blessed Trinity. Mary epitomizes such participation in the life of God. Her response was not made without profound questioning, and it issued in a life of joy intermingled with sorrow, taking her even to the foot of her son's cross. When Christians join in Mary's 'Amen' to the 'Yes' of God in Christ, they commit themselves to an obedient response to the Word of God, which leads to a life of prayer and service. Like Mary, they not only magnify the Lord with their lips: they commit themselves to serve God's justice with their lives (cf. Luke 1:46–55).

A MARY ACCORDING TO THE SCRIPTURES

6 We remain convinced that the holy Scriptures, as the Word of God written, bear normative witness to God's plan of salvation, so it is to them that this statement first turns. Indeed, it is impossible to be faithful to Scripture and not to take Mary seriously. We recognize, however, that for some centuries Anglicans and Roman Catholics have interpreted the Scriptures while divided from one another. In reflecting together on the Scriptures' testimony concerning Mary, we have discovered more than just a few tantalizing

glimpses into the life of a great saint. We have found ourselves meditating with wonder and gratitude on the whole sweep of salvation history: creation, election, the Incarnation, passion, and resurrection of Christ, the gift of the Spirit in the Church, and the final vision of eternal life for all God's people in the new creation.

7   In the following paragraphs, our use of Scripture seeks to draw upon the whole tradition of the Church, in which rich and varied readings have been employed. In the New Testament, the Old Testament is commonly interpreted typologically[1]: events and images are understood with specific reference to Christ. This approach is further developed by the Fathers and by medieval preachers and authors. The Reformers stressed the clarity and sufficiency of Scripture, and called for a return to the centrality of the Gospel message. Historical-critical approaches

---

1. By typology we mean a reading which accepts that certain things in Scripture (persons, places, and events) foreshadow or illuminate other things, or reflect patterns of faith in imaginative ways (e.g. Adam is a type of Christ: Romans 5:14; Isaiah 7:14 points towards the virgin birth of Jesus: Matthew 1:23). This typological sense was considered to be a meaning that goes beyond the literal sense. This approach assumes the unity and consistency of the divine revelation.

attempted to discern the meaning intended by the biblical authors, and to account for texts' origins. Each of these readings has its limitations, and may give rise to exaggerations or imbalances: typology can become extravagant, Reformation emphases reductionist, and critical methods overly historicist. More recent approaches to Scripture point to the range of possible readings of a text, notably its narrative, rhetorical, and sociological dimensions. In this statement, we seek to integrate what is valuable from each of these approaches, as both correcting and contributing to our use of Scripture. Further, we recognize that no reading of a text is neutral, but each is shaped by the context and interest of its readers. Our reading has taken place within the context of our dialogue in Christ, for the sake of that communion which is his will. It is thus an ecclesial and ecumenical reading, seeking to consider each passage about Mary in the context of the New Testament as a whole, against the background of the Old, and in the light of Tradition.

The Witness of Scripture: A Trajectory of Grace and Hope

8 The Old Testament bears witness to God's creation of men and women in the divine image, and God's

loving call to covenant relationship with himself. Even when they disobeyed, God did not abandon human beings to sin and the power of death. Again and again God offered a covenant of grace. God made a covenant with Noah that never again would "all flesh" be destroyed by the waters of a flood. The Lord made a covenant with Abraham that, through him, all the families of the earth might be blessed. Through Moses he made a covenant with Israel that, obedient to his word, they might be a holy nation and a priestly people. The prophets repeatedly summoned the people to turn back from disobedience to the gracious God of the covenant, to receive God's word and let it bear fruit in their lives. They looked forward to a renewal of the covenant in which there would be perfect obedience and perfect self-giving: "This is the covenant that I will make with the house of Israel after those days, says the LORD: I will put my law within them, and I will write it on their hearts; and I will be their God, and they shall be my people" (Jeremiah 31:33). In the prophecy of Ezekiel, this hope is spoken of not only in terms of washing and cleansing, but also of the gift of the Spirit (Ezekiel 36:25–28).

9 The covenant between the Lord and his people is several times described as a love affair between God

and Israel, the virgin daughter of Zion, bride and mother: "I gave you my solemn oath and entered into a covenant with you, declares the Sovereign Lord, and you became mine" (Ezekiel 16:8; cf. Isaiah 54:1 and Galatians 4:27). Even in punishing faithlessness, God remains forever faithful, promising to restore the covenant relationship and to draw together the scattered people (Hosea 1–2; Jeremiah 2:2, 31:3; Isaiah 62:4–5). Nuptial imagery is also used within the New Testament to describe the relationship between Christ and the Church (Ephesians 5:21–33; Revelation 21:9). In parallel to the prophetic image of Israel as the bride of the Lord, the Solomonic literature of the Old Testament characterizes Holy Wisdom as the handmaid of the Lord (Proverbs 8:22f; cf. Wisdom 7:22–26) similarly emphasizing the theme of responsiveness and creative activity. In the New Testament these prophetic and wisdom motifs are combined (Luke 11:49) and fulfilled in the coming of Christ.

10 The Scriptures also speak of the calling by God of particular persons, such as David, Elijah, Jeremiah, and Isaiah, so that within the people of God certain special tasks may be performed. They bear witness to the gift of the Spirit or the presence of God enabling them to accomplish God's will and purpose. There

are also profound reflections on what it is to be known and called by God from the very beginning of one's existence (Psalm 139:13–16; Jeremiah 1:4–5). This sense of wonder at the prevenient grace of God is similarly attested in the New Testament, especially in the writings of Paul, when he speaks of those who are "called according to God's purpose," affirming that those whom God "foreknew he also predestined to be conformed to the image of his Son . . . And those whom he predestined he also called; and those whom he called he also justified; and those whom he justified he also glorified" (Romans 8:28–30; cf. 2 Timothy 1:9). The preparation by God for a prophetic task is exemplified in the words spoken by the angel to Zechariah before the birth of John the Baptist: "He will be filled with the Holy Spirit, even from his mother's womb" (Luke 1:15; cf. Judges 13:3–5).

11 Following through the trajectory of the grace of God and the hope for a perfect human response which we have traced in the preceding paragraphs, Christians have, in line with the New Testament writers, seen its culmination in the obedience of Christ. Within this Christological context, they have discerned a similar pattern in the one who would

receive the Word in her heart and in her body, be overshadowed by the Spirit and give birth to the Son of God. The New Testament speaks not only of God's preparation for the birth of the Son, but also of God's election, calling, and sanctification of a Jewish woman in the line of those holy women, such as Sarah and Hannah, whose sons fulfilled the purposes of God for his people. Paul speaks of the Son of God being born "in the fullness of time" and "born of a woman, born under the Law" (Galatians 4:4). The birth of Mary's son is the fulfilment of God's will for Israel, and Mary's part in that fulfilment is that of free and unqualified consent in utter self-giving and trust: "Behold I am the handmaid of the Lord; let it be done to me according to your word" (Luke 1:38; cf. Psalm 123:2).

Mary in Matthew's Birth Narrative

12 While various parts of the New Testament refer to the birth of Christ, only two Gospels, Matthew and Luke, each from its own perspective, narrate the story of his birth and refer specifically to Mary. Matthew entitles his book "the Genesis of Jesus Christ" (1:1) echoing the way the Bible begins (Genesis 1:1). In the genealogy (1:1–18), he traces the genesis of Jesus

back through the Exile to David and ultimately to Abraham. He notes the unlikely role played in the providential ordering of Israel's salvation history by four women, each of whom stretches the boundaries of the Covenant. This emphasis on continuity with the old is counter-balanced in the following account of Jesus' birth by an emphasis on the new (cf. 9:17), a type of re-creation by the Holy Spirit, revealing new possibilities of salvation from sin (1:21) and of the presence of "God with us" (1:23). Matthew stretches the boundaries further in holding together Jesus' Davidic descent through the legal fatherhood of Joseph, and his birth from the Virgin according to Isaiah's prophecy—"Behold a virgin shall conceive and bear a son" (Isaiah 7:14 LXX).

13 In Matthew's account, Mary is mentioned in con-junction with her son in such phrases as "Mary his mother" or "the child and his mother" (2:11, 13, 20, 21). Amid all the political intrigue, murder, and dis-placement of this tale, one quiet moment of rever-ence has captured the Christian imagination: the Magi, whose profession it is to know when the time has come, kneel in homage to the infant King with his royal mother (2:2, 11). Matthew emphasizes the continuity of Jesus Christ with Israel's messianic

expectation and the newness that comes with the birth of the Saviour. Descent from David by whatever route, and birth at the ancestral royal city, disclose the first. The virginal conception discloses the second.

Mary in Luke's Birth Narrative

14 In Luke's infancy narrative, Mary is prominent from the beginning. She is the link between John the Baptist and Jesus, whose miraculous births are laid out in deliberate parallel. She receives the angel's message and responds in humble obedience (1:38). She travels on her own from Galilee to Judaea to visit Elizabeth (1:40) and in her song proclaims the eschatological reversal which will be at the heart of her son's proclamation of the Kingdom of God. Mary is the one who in recollection looks beneath the surface of events (2:19, 51) and represents the inwardness of faith and suffering (2:35). She speaks on Joseph's behalf in the scene at the Temple and, although chided for her initial incomprehension, continues to grow in understanding (2:48–51).

15 Within the Lucan narrative, two particular scenes invite reflection on the place of Mary in the life of the Church: the Annunciation and the visit to Elizabeth.

These passages emphasize that Mary is in a unique way the recipient of God's election and grace. The Annunciation story recapitulates several incidents in the Old Testament, notably the births of Isaac (Genesis 18:10–14), Samson (Judges 13:2–5) and Samuel (1 Samuel 1:1–20). The angel's greeting also evokes the passages in Isaiah (66:7–11), Zechariah (9:9), and Zephaniah (3:14–17) that call on the "Daughter of Zion", i.e., Israel awaiting with joy the arrival of her Lord. The choice of 'overshadow' (*episkiasei*) to describe the action of the Holy Spirit in the virginal conception (Luke 1:35) echoes the cherubim overshadowing the Ark of the Covenant (Exodus 25:20), the presence of God overshadowing the Tabernacle (Exodus 40:35), and the brooding of the Spirit over the waters at the creation (Genesis 1:2). At the Visitation, Mary's song (*Magnificat*) mirrors the song of Hannah (1 Samuel 2:1–10), broadening its scope so that Mary becomes the one who speaks for all the poor and oppressed who long for God's reign of justice to be established. Just as in Elizabeth's salutation the mother receives a blessing of her own, distinct from that of her child (1:42), so also in the *Magnificat* Mary predicts that "all generations will call me blessed" (1:48). This text provides the scriptural basis for an appropriate devotion to

Mary, though never in separation from her role as mother of the Messiah.

16 In the Annunciation story, the angel calls Mary the Lord's "favoured one" (Greek *kecharitōmenē*, a perfect participle meaning 'one who has been and remains endowed with grace') in a way that implies a prior sanctification by divine grace with a view to her calling. The angel's announcement connects Jesus' being "holy" and "Son of God" with his conception by the Holy Spirit (1:35). The virginal conception then points to the divine sonship of the Saviour who will be born of Mary. The infant not yet born is described by Elizabeth as the Lord: "And why is this granted to me that the mother of my Lord should come to me?" (1:43). The trinitarian pattern of divine action in these scenes is striking: the Incarnation of the Son is initiated by the Father's election of the Blessed Virgin and is mediated by the Holy Spirit. Equally striking is Mary's *fiat*, her 'Amen' given in faith and freedom to God's powerful Word communicated by the angel (1:38).

17 In Luke's account of the birth of Jesus, the praise offered to God by the shepherds parallels the Magi's adoration of the infant in Matthew's account. Again,

this is the scene that constitutes the still centre at the heart of the birth story: "They found Mary and Joseph and the baby lying in a manger" (Luke 2:16). In accordance with the Law of Moses, the baby is circumcised and presented in the Temple. On this occasion, Simeon has a special word of prophecy for the mother of the Christ-child, that "a sword will pierce your soul" (Luke 2:34–35). From this point on Mary's pilgrimage of faith leads to the foot of the cross.

The Virginal Conception

18 The divine initiative in human history is proclaimed in the good news of the virginal conception through the action of the Holy Spirit (Matthew 1:20–23; Luke 1:34–35). The virginal conception may appear in the first place as an absence, i.e. the absence of a human father. It is in reality, however, a sign of the presence and work of the Spirit. Belief in the virginal conception is an early Christian tradition adopted and developed independently by Matthew and Luke.[2] For Christian believers, it is an eloquent sign

---

2 . Given its strongly Jewish matrix in both Matthean and Lucan versions, an appeal to analogies with pagan mythology or to an exaltation of virginity over the married state to explain the origin of the tradition

of the divine sonship of Christ and of new life through the Spirit. The virginal conception also points to the new birth of every Christian, as an adopted child of God. Each is "born again (from above) by water and the Spirit" (John 3:3–5). Seen in this light, the virginal conception, far from being an isolated miracle, is a powerful expression of what the Church believes about her Lord, and about our salvation.

Mary and the True Family of Jesus

19 After these birth stories, it comes as something of a surprise to read the episode, narrated in all three Synoptic Gospels, which addresses the question of Jesus' true family. Mark tells us that Jesus' "mother and his brother" (Mark 3:31) come and stand outside, wanting to speak to him.[3] Jesus in response distances

---

is implausible. Nor is the idea of virginal conception likely to derive from an over-literal reading of the Greek text of Isaiah 7:14 (LXX), for that is not the way the idea is introduced in the Lucan account. Moreover, the suggestion that it originated as an answer to the accusation of illegitimacy levelled at Jesus is unlikely, as that accusation could equally have arisen because it was known that there was something unusual about Jesus' birth (cf. Mark 6:3; John 8:41) and because of the Church's claim about his virginal conception.

3. Although the word 'brother' usually denotes a blood brother, the Greek *adelphos*, like the Hebrew *'ah*, can have a broader meaning of kinsman, or relative (e.g. Genesis 29:12 LXX) or step-brother (e.g. Mark

himself from his natural family: he speaks instead of those gathered around him, his 'eschatological family', that is to say, "whoever does the will of God" (3:35). For Mark, Jesus' natural family, including his own mother, seems at this stage to lack understanding of the true nature of his mission. But that will be the case also with his disciples (e.g. 8:33–35, 9:30–33, 10:35–40). Mark indicates that growth in understanding is inevitably slow and painful, and that genuine faith in Christ is not reached until the encounter with the cross and the empty tomb.

20 In Luke, the stark contrast between the attitude towards Jesus of his natural and eschatological family is avoided (Luke 8:19–21). In a later scene (11:27–28), the woman in the crowd who utters a blessing on his mother, "Blessed is the womb that bore you and the breasts that you sucked", is corrected: "Blessed rather are those who hear the word of God and keep it." But that form of blessing, as Luke sees it, definitely includes Mary who, from the

---

6:17f). Relatives who are not siblings could be included in this use of the term at Mark 3:31. Mary did have an extended family: her sister is referred to at John 19:25 and her kinswoman Elizabeth at Luke 1:36. In the early Church different explanations of the references to the 'brothers' of Jesus were given, whether as step-brothers or cousins.

beginning of his account, was ready to let everything in her life happen according to God's word (1:38).

21 In his second book, the Acts of the Apostles, Luke notes that between the ascension of the Risen Lord and the feast of Pentecost the apostles were gathered in Jerusalem "together with the women and Mary the mother of Jesus, and with his brothers" (Acts 1:14). Mary, who was receptive to the working of God's Spirit at the birth of the Messiah (Luke 1:35–38), is here part of the community of disciples waiting in prayer for the outpouring of the Spirit at the birth of the Church.

Mary in John's Gospel

22 Mary is not mentioned explicitly in the Prologue of John's Gospel. However, something of the significance of her role in salvation history may be discerned by placing her in the context of the considered theological truths that the evangelist articulates in unfolding the good news of the Incarnation. The theological emphasis on the divine initiative, that in the narratives of Matthew and Luke is expressed in the story of Jesus' birth, is paralleled in the Prologue of John by an emphasis on the

predestining will and grace of God by which all those who are brought to new birth are said to be born "not of blood, nor of the will of the flesh, nor of the will of man, but of God" (1:13). These are words that could be applied to the birth of Jesus himself.

23 At two important moments of Jesus' public life, the beginning (the wedding at Cana) and the end (the Cross), John notes the presence of Jesus' mother. Each is an hour of need: the first on the surface rather trivial, but at a deeper level a symbolic anticipation of the second. John gives a prominent position in his Gospel to the wedding at Cana (2:1–12), calling it the beginning (*archē*) of the signs of Jesus. The account emphasizes the new wine which Jesus brings, symbolizing the eschatological marriage feast of God with his people and the messianic banquet of the Kingdom. The story primarily conveys a Christological message: Jesus reveals his messianic glory to his disciples and they believe in him (2:11).

24 The presence of the "mother of Jesus" is mentioned at the beginning of the story: she has a distinctive role in the unfolding of the narrative. Mary seems to

have been invited and be present in her own right, not with "Jesus and his disciples" (2:1–2); Jesus is initially seen as present as part of his mother's family. In the dialogue between them when the wine runs out, Jesus seems at first to refuse Mary's implied request, but in the end he accedes to it. This reading of the narrative, however, leaves room for a deeper symbolic reading of the event. In Mary's words "they have no wine", John ascribes to her the expression not so much of a deficiency in the wedding arrangements, as of the longing for salvation of the whole covenant people, who have water for purification but lack the joyful wine of the messianic kingdom. In his answer, Jesus begins by calling into question his former relationship with his mother ("What is there between you and me?"), implying that a change has to take place. He does not address Mary as 'mother', but as "woman" (cf. John 19:26). Jesus no longer sees his relation to Mary as simply one of earthly kinship.

25 Mary's response, to instruct the servants to "Do whatever he tells you" (2:5), is unexpected; she is not in charge of the feast (cf. 2:8). Her initial role as the mother of Jesus has radically changed. She herself is now seen as a believer within the messianic community. From this moment on, she commits herself

totally to the Messiah and his word. A new relationship results, indicated by the change in the order of
the main characters at the end of the story: "After
this he went down to Capernaum, with his mother
and his brothers and his disciples" (2:12). The Cana
narrative opens by placing Jesus within the family of
Mary, his mother; from now on, Mary is part of the
"company of Jesus", his disciple. Our reading of this
passage reflects the Church's understanding of the
role of Mary: to help the disciples come to her son,
Jesus Christ, and to "do whatever he tells you."

26 John's second mention of the presence of Mary
occurs at the decisive hour of Jesus' messianic mission,
his crucifixion (19:25–27). Standing with other disciples at the cross, Mary shares in the suffering of ·
Jesus, who in his last moments addresses a special
word to her, "Woman, behold your son", and to the
beloved disciple, "Behold your mother." We cannot
but be touched that, even in his dying moments,
Jesus is concerned for the welfare of his mother,
showing his filial affection. This surface reading
again invites a symbolic and ecclesial reading of
John's rich narrative. These last commands of Jesus
before he dies reveal an understanding beyond
their primary reference to Mary and "the beloved

disciple" as individuals. The reciprocal roles of the 'woman' and the 'disciple' are related to the identity of the Church. Elsewhere in John, the beloved disciple is presented as the model disciple of Jesus, the one closest to him who never deserted him, the object of Jesus' love, and the ever-faithful witness (13:25, 19:26, 20:1–10, 21:20–25). Understood in terms of discipleship, Jesus' dying words give Mary a motherly role in the Church and encourage the community of disciples to embrace her as a spiritual mother.

27 A corporate understanding of 'woman' also calls the Church constantly to behold Christ crucified, and calls each disciple to care for the Church as mother. Implicit here perhaps is a Mary-Eve typology: just as the first 'woman' was taken from Adam's 'rib' (Genesis 2:22, *pleura* LXX) and became the mother of all the living (Genesis 3:20), so the 'woman' Mary is, on a spiritual level, the mother of all who gain true life from the water and blood that flow from the side (Greek *pleura*, literally 'rib') of Christ (19:34) and from the Spirit that is breathed out from his triumphant sacrifice (19:30, 20:22, cf. 1 John 5:8). In such symbolic and corporate readings, images for the Church, Mary, and discipleship interact with one

another. Mary is seen as the personification of Israel, now giving birth to the Christian community (cf. Isaiah 54:1, 66:7–8), just as she had given birth earlier to the Messiah (cf. Isaiah 7:14). When John's account of Mary at the beginning and end of Jesus' ministry is viewed in this light, it is difficult to speak of the Church without thinking of Mary, the Mother of the Lord, as its archetype and first realization.

The Woman in Revelation 12

28 In highly symbolic language, full of scriptural imagery, the seer of Revelation describes the vision of a sign in heaven involving a woman, a dragon, and the woman's child. The narrative of Revelation 12 serves to assure the reader of the ultimate victory of God's faithful ones in times of persecution and eschatological struggle. In the course of history, the symbol of the woman has led to a variety of interpretations. Most scholars accept that the primary meaning of the woman is corporate: the people of God, whether Israel, the Church of Christ, or both. Moreover, the narrative style of the author suggests that the 'full picture' of the woman is attained only at the end of the book when the Church of Christ becomes the triumphant New Jerusalem (Revelation 21:1–3). The

actual troubles of the author's community are placed in the frame of history as a whole, which is the scene of the ongoing struggle between the faithful and their enemies, between good and evil, between God and Satan. The imagery of the offspring reminds us of the struggle in Genesis 3:15 between the serpent and the woman, between the serpent's seed and the woman's seed.[4]

29 Given this primary ecclesial interpretation of Revelation 12, is it still possible to find in it a secondary reference to Mary? The text does not explicitly identify the woman with Mary. It refers to the woman as the mother of the "male child who is to rule all the nations with a rod of iron", a citation from

---

4. The Hebrew text of Genesis 3:15 speaks about enmity between the serpent and the woman, and between the offspring of both. The personal pronoun (*hu'*) in the words addressed to the serpent, "He will strike at your head," is masculine. In the Greek translation used by the early Church (LXX), however, the personal pronoun *autos* (he) cannot refer to the offspring (neuter: *to sperma*), but must refer to a masculine individual who could then be the Messiah, born of a woman. The Vulgate (mis)translates the clause as *ipsa conteret caput tuum* ("she will strike at your head"). This feminine pronoun supported a reading of this passage as referring to Mary which has become traditional in the Latin Church. The Neo-Vulgate (1986), however, returns to the neuter *ipsum*, which refers to *semen illius*: "*Inimicitias ponam inter te et mulierem et semen tuum et semen illius; ipsum conteret caput tuum, et tu conteres calcaneum eius.*"

Psalm 2 elsewhere in the New Testament applied to
the Messiah as well as to the faithful people of God
(cf. Hebrews 1:5, 5:5, Acts 13:33 with Revelation
2:27). In view of this, some Patristic writers came to
think of the mother of Jesus when reading this chapter.[5] Given the place of the book of Revelation
within the canon of Scripture, in which the different
biblical images intertwine, the possibility arose of a
more explicit interpretation, both individual and
corporate, of Revelation 12, illuminating the place of
Mary and the Church in the eschatological victory
of the Messiah.

Scriptural Reflection

30 The scriptural witness summons all believers in every
generation to call Mary 'blessed'; this Jewish woman
of humble status, this daughter of Israel living in
hope of justice for the poor, whom God has graced
and chosen to become the virgin mother of his Son
through the overshadowing of the Holy Spirit. We
are to bless her as the 'handmaid of the Lord' who

---

5. Cf. Epiphanius of Salamis (†402), *Panarion* 78.11; Quodvultdeus
(†454) *Sermones de Symbolo* III, I.4–6; Oecumenius (†c.550)
Commentarius in Apocalypsin 6.

gave her unqualified assent to the fulfilment of God's saving plan, as the mother who pondered all things in her heart, as the refugee seeking asylum in a foreign land, as the mother pierced by the innocent suffering of her own child, and as the woman to whom Jesus entrusted his friends. We are at one with her and the apostles, as they pray for the outpouring of the Spirit upon the nascent Church, the eschatological family of Christ. And we may even glimpse in her the final destiny of God's people to share in her son's victory over the powers of evil and death.

B MARY IN THE CHRISTIAN TRADITION

Christ and Mary in the Ancient Common Tradition

31 In the early Church, reflection on Mary served to interpret and safeguard the apostolic Tradition centred on Jesus Christ. Patristic testimony to Mary as 'God-bearer' (*Theotókos*) emerged from reflection on Scripture and the celebration of Christian feasts, but its development was due chiefly to the early Christological controversies. In the crucible of these controversies of the first five centuries, and their resolution in successive Ecumenical Councils, reflection

on Mary's role in the Incarnation was integral to the articulation of orthodox faith in Jesus Christ, true God and true man.

32 In defence of Christ's true humanity, and against Docetism, the early Church emphasized Jesus' birth from Mary. He did not just 'appear' to be human; he did not descend from heaven in a 'heavenly body', nor when he was born did he simply 'pass through' his mother. Rather, Mary gave birth to her son of her own substance. For Ignatius of Antioch (†c.110) and Tertullian (†c.225), Jesus is fully human, because 'truly born' of Mary. In the words of the Nicaeo-Constantinopolitan Creed (381), "he was incarnate of the Holy Spirit and the Virgin Mary, and was made man." The definition of Chalcedon (451), reaffirming this creed, attests that Christ is "consubstantial with the Father according to the divinity and consubstantial with us according to the humanity." The Athanasian Creed confesses yet more concretely that he is "man, of the substance of his Mother." This Anglicans and Roman Catholics together affirm.

33 In defence of his true divinity, the early Church emphasized Mary's virginal conception of Jesus Christ. According to the Fathers, his conception by

the Holy Spirit testifies to Christ's divine origin and divine identity. The One born of Mary is the eternal Son of God. Eastern and Western Fathers—such as Justin (†c.150), Irenaeus (†c.202), Athanasius (†373), and Ambrose (†397)—expounded this New Testament teaching in terms of Genesis 3 (Mary is the antitype of 'virgin Eve') and Isaiah 7:14 (she fulfils the prophet's vision and gives birth to "God with us"). They appealed to the virginal conception to defend both the Lord's divinity and Mary's honour. As the Apostles' Creed confesses: Jesus Christ was "conceived by the Holy Spirit and born of the Virgin Mary." This Anglicans and Roman Catholics together affirm.

34 Mary's title *Theotókos* was formally invoked to safeguard the orthodox doctrine of the unity of Christ's person. This title had been in use in churches under the influence of Alexandria at least from the time of the Arian controversy. Since Jesus Christ is "true God from true God", as the Council of Nicaea (325) declared, these churches concluded that his mother, Mary, can rightly be called the 'God-bearer'. Churches under the influence of Antioch, however, conscious of the threat Apollinarianism posed to belief in the full humanity of Christ, did not immediately adopt this title. The debate between Cyril of

Alexandria (†444) and Nestorius (†455), patriarch of Constantinople, who was formed in the Antiochene school, revealed that the real issue in the question of Mary's title was the unity of Christ's person. The ensuing Council of Ephesus (431) used *Theotókos* (literally 'God-bearer'; in Latin, *Deipara*) to affirm the oneness of Christ's person by identifying Mary as the Mother of God the Word incarnate.[6] The rule of faith on this matter takes more precise expression in the definition of Chalcedon: "One and the same Son ... was begotten from the Father before the ages as to the divinity and in the latter days for us and our salvation was born as to the humanity from Mary the Virgin *Theotókos*." In receiving the Council of Ephesus and the definition of Chalcedon, Anglicans and Roman Catholics together confess Mary as *Theotókos*.

The Celebration of Mary in the Ancient Common Traditions

35 In the early centuries, communion in Christ included a strong sense of the living presence of the saints as an integral part of the spiritual experience of the

---

6. The Council solemnly approved the content of the Second Letter of Cyril to Nestorius: "It was not that an ordinary man was born first of the holy Virgin, on whom afterwards the Word descended; what we say

churches (Hebrews 12:1, 22–24; Revelation 6:9–11; 7; 8:3–4). Within the 'cloud of witnesses', the Lord's mother came to be seen to have a special place. Themes developed from Scripture and in devotional reflection reveal a deep awareness of Mary's role in the redemption of humanity. Such themes include Mary as Eve's counterpart and as a type of the Church. The response of Christian people, reflecting on these themes, found devotional expression in both private and public prayer.

36 Exegetes delighted in drawing feminine imagery from the Scriptures to contemplate the significance both of the Church and Mary. Fathers as early as Justin Martyr (†c.150) and Irenaeus (†c.202), reflecting on texts like Genesis 3 and Luke 1:26–38, developed, alongside the antithesis of Adam/New Adam, that of Eve/New Eve. Just as Eve is associated with Adam in bringing about our defeat, so Mary is associated with her Son in the conquest of the ancient enemy (cf. Genesis 3:15, *vide supra* footnote 4): 'virgin' Eve's disobedience results in death; the virgin

---

is that: being united with the flesh from the womb, the Word has undergone birth in the flesh. . . therefore the Holy Fathers had the courage to call the Holy Virgin *Theotókos*"(DS 251).

Mary's obedience opens the way to salvation. The New Eve shares in the New Adam's victory over sin and death.

37 The Fathers presented Mary the Virgin Mother as a model of holiness for consecrated virgins, and increasingly taught that she had remained 'Ever-Virgin'.[7] In their reflection, virginity was understood not only as physical integrity, but as an interior disposition of openness, obedience, and single-hearted fidelity to Christ which models Christian discipleship and issues in spiritual fruitfulness.

38 In this patristic understanding, Mary's virginity was closely related to her sanctity. Although some early

---

7. The Tome of Leo, which was decisive for the outcome of the Council of Chalcedon (451), states that Christ "was conceived by the Holy Spirit in the womb of the Virgin Mother, who gave him birth without losing her virginity, as she conceived him without losing her virginity" (DS 291). Similarly Athanasius speaks in *De Virginitate* (*Le Muséon* 42: 244.248) of "Mary, who . . . remained a virgin to the end [as a model for] all to come after her." Cf. John Chrysostom (†407) *Homily on Matthew* 5,3. The first Ecumenical Council to use the term *Aeiparthenos* (*semper virgo*) was the Second Council of Constantinople (553). This designation is already implicit in the classical Western formulation of Mary's *virginitas as ante partum, in partu, post partum*. This tradition appears consistently in the western Church from Ambrose onward. As Augustine wrote, "she conceived him as a virgin, she gave birth as a virgin, she remained a virgin" (*Sermo* 51.18; cf. *Sermo* 196.1).

exegetes thought that Mary was not wholly without sin,[8] Augustine (†430) witnessed to contemporary reluctance to speak of any sin in her.

> We must except the holy Virgin Mary, concerning whom I wish to raise no question when it touches the subject of sins, out of honour to the Lord; for from him we know what abundance of grace for overcoming sin in every particular was conferred on her who had the merit to conceive and bear him who undoubtedly had no sin. (*De natura et gratia* 36.42)

Other Fathers from West and East, appealing to the angelic salutation (Luke 1:28) and Mary's response (Luke 1:38), support the view that Mary was filled with grace from her origin in anticipation of her unique vocation as Mother of the Lord. By the fifth century they hail her as a new creation: blameless, spotless, "holy in body and soul" (Theodotus of Ancyra, *Homily* 6, 11: †before 446). By the sixth

---

8. Thus Irenaeus criticises her for "excessive haste" at Cana, "seeking to push her son into performing a miracle before his hour had come" (*Adversus Haereses* III.16.7); Origen speaks of her wavering in faith at the cross, "so she too would have some sin for which Christ died" (*Homilia in Lucam*, 17,6). Suggestions like these are found in the writings of Tertullian, Ambrose, and John Chrysostom.

century, the title *panaghia* ('all-holy') can be found in the East.

39 Following the Christological debates at the councils of Ephesus and Chalcedon, devotion to Mary flourished. When the patriarch of Antioch refused Mary the title of *Theotókos*, Emperor Leo I (457–474) commanded the patriarch of Constantinople to insert this title into the eucharistic prayer throughout the East. By the sixth century, commemoration of Mary as 'God-bearer' had become universal in the eucharistic prayers of East and West (with the exception of the Assyrian Church of the East). Texts and images celebrating Mary's holiness were multiplied in liturgical poetry and songs, such as the *Akathist*, a hymn probably written soon after Chalcedon and still sung in the Eastern church. A tradition of praying with and praising Mary was thus gradually established. This has been associated since the fourth century, especially in the East, with asking for her protection.[9]

---

9. Witness the invocation of Mary in the early text known traditionally as *Sub tuum praesidium*: Ὑπὸ τὴν σὴν εὐσπλαγνίαν καταφεύγομεν, Θεοτόκε τὰς ἡμῶν ἱκεσίας μὴ παρίδῃς ἐν περιστάσει, ἀλλ' ἐκ κινδύνου ῥῦσαι ἡμᾶς, μόνη ἁγνή, μόνη εὐλογημένη. (Cf. O. Stegemüller, *Sub tuum praesidium. Bemerkungen zur ältesten Überlieferung*, in: *ZKTh* 74 [1952], pp.76–82 [77]). This text (with two changes) is used to this day in the

40 After the Council of Ephesus, churches began to be dedicated to Mary and feasts in her honour began to be celebrated on particular days in these churches. Prompted by popular piety and gradually adopted by local churches, feasts celebrating Mary's conception (December 8/9), birth (September 8), presentation (November 21), and dormition (August 15) mirrored the liturgical commemorations of events in the life of the Lord. They drew both on the canonical Scriptures and also on apocryphal accounts of Mary's early life and her 'falling asleep'. A feast of the conception of Mary can be dated in the East to the late seventh century, and was introduced into the Western church through southern England in the early eleventh century. It drew on popular devotion expressed in the second-century *Protoevangelium of James*, and paralleled the dominical feast of the Annunciation and the existing feast of the conception of John the Baptist. The feast of Mary's 'falling asleep' dates from the end of the sixth century, but

---

Greek liturgical tradition; versions of this prayer also occur in the Ambrosian, Roman, Byzantine, and Coptic liturgies. A familiar English version is: "We fly to thy protection, O holy Mother of God; despise not our petitions in our necessities but deliver us from all dangers, O ever glorious and blessed Virgin."

was influenced by legendary narratives of the end of Mary's life already widely in circulation. In the West, the most influential of them are the *Transitus Mariae*. In the East, the feast was known as the 'dormition', which implied her death but did not exclude her being taken into heaven. In the West, the term used was 'assumption', which emphasized her being taken into heaven but did not exclude the possibility of her dying. Belief in her assumption was grounded in the promise of the resurrection of the dead and the recognition of Mary's dignity as *Theotókos* and 'Ever Virgin', coupled with the conviction that she who had borne Life should be associated to her Son's victory over death, and with the glorification of his Body, the Church.

The Growth of Marian Doctrine and Devotion in the Middle Ages

41 The spread of these feasts of Mary gave rise to homilies in which preachers delved into the Scriptures, searching for types and motifs to illuminate the Virgin's place in the economy of salvation. During the High Middle Ages a growing emphasis on the humanity of Christ was matched by attention to the exemplary virtues of Mary. Bernard, for example,

articulates this emphasis in his homilies. Meditation on the lives of both Christ and Mary became increasingly popular, and gave rise to the development of such devotional practices as the rosary. The paintings, sculptures, and stained glass of the High and Late Middle Ages lent to this devotion immediacy and colour.

42 During these centuries there were some major shifts of emphasis in theological reflection about Mary. Theologians of the High Middle Ages developed patristic reflection on Mary as a 'type' of the Church, and also as the New Eve, in a way that associated her ever more closely with Christ in the continuing work of redemption. The centre of attention of believers shifted from Mary as representing the faithful Church, and so also redeemed humanity, to Mary as dispensing Christ's graces to the faithful. Scholastic theologians in the West developed an increasingly elaborate body of doctrine about Mary in her own right. Much of this doctrine grew out of speculation about the holiness and sanctification of Mary. Questions about this were influenced not only by the scholastic theology of grace and original sin, but also by presuppositions concerning procreation and the relation between soul and body. For example,

if she were sanctified in the womb of her mother, more perfectly even than John the Baptist and Jeremiah, some theologians thought that the precise moment of her sanctification had to be determined according to the current understanding of when the 'rational soul' was infused into the body. Theological developments in the Western doctrine of grace and sin raised other questions: how could Mary be free of all sin, including original sin, without jeopardising the role of Christ as universal Saviour? Speculative reflection led to intense discussions about how Christ's redeeming grace may have preserved Mary from original sin. The measured theology of Mary's sanctification found in the *Summa Theologiae* of Thomas Aquinas, and the subtle reasoning of Duns Scotus about Mary, were deployed in extended controversy over whether Mary was immaculate from the first moment of her conception.

43 In the Late Middle Ages, scholastic theology grew increasingly apart from spirituality. Less and less rooted in scriptural exegesis, theologians relied on logical probability to establish their positions, and Nominalists speculated on what could be done by the absolute power and will of God. Spirituality, no longer in creative tension with theology, emphasized

affectivity and personal experience. In popular religion, Mary came widely to be viewed as an intermediary between God and humanity, and even as a worker of miracles with powers that verged on the divine. This popular piety in due course influenced the theological opinions of those who had grown up with it, and who subsequently elaborated a theological rationale for the florid Marian devotion of the Late Middle Ages.

From the Reformation to the Present Day

44 One powerful impulse for Reformation in the early sixteenth century was a widespread reaction against devotional practices which approached Mary as a mediatrix alongside Christ, or sometimes even in his place. Such exaggerated devotions, in part inspired by presentations of Christ as inaccessible Judge as well as Redeemer, were sharply criticized by Erasmus and Thomas More and decisively rejected by the Reformers. Together with a radical re-reception of Scripture as the fundamental touchstone of divine revelation, there was a re-reception by the Reformers of the belief that Jesus Christ is the only mediator between God and humanity. This entailed a rejection of real and perceived abuses surrounding devotion to

Mary. It led also to the loss of some positive aspects of devotion and the diminution of her place in the life of the Church.

45 In this context, the English Reformers continued to receive the doctrine of the ancient Church concerning Mary. Their positive teaching about Mary concentrated on her role in the Incarnation: it is summed up in their acceptance of her as the *Theotókos*, because this was seen to be both scriptural and in accord with ancient common tradition. Following the traditions of the early Church and other Reformers like Martin Luther, the English Reformers such as Latimer (*Works*, 2:105), Cranmer (*Works*, 2:60; 2:88), and Jewel (*Works*, 3:440–441) accepted that Mary was 'Ever Virgin'. Following Augustine, they showed a reticence about affirming that Mary was a sinner. Their chief concern was to emphasize the unique sinlessness of Christ, and the need of all humankind, including Mary, for a Saviour (cf. Luke 1:47). Articles IX and XV affirmed the universality of human sinfulness. They neither affirmed nor denied the possibility of Mary having been preserved by grace from participation in this general human condition. It is notable that the *Book of Common Prayer* in the Christmas collect and preface refers to Mary as 'a pure virgin'.

46 From 1561, the calendar of the Church of England (which was reproduced in the 1662 *Book of Common Prayer*) contained five feasts associated with Mary: Conception of Mary, Nativity of Mary, Annunciation, Visitation, and Purification/Presentation. There was, however, no longer a feast of the Assumption (August 15): not only was it understood to lack scriptural warrant, but was also seen as exalting Mary at the expense of Christ. Anglican liturgy, as expressed in the successive *Books of Common Prayer* (1549, 1552, 1559, 1662) when it mentions Mary, gives prominence to her role as the 'pure Virgin' from whose 'substance' the Son took human nature (cf. Article II). In spite of the diminution of devotion to Mary in the sixteenth century, reverence for her endured in the continued use of the *Magnificat* in Evening Prayer, and the unchanged dedication of ancient churches and Lady Chapels. In the seventeenth century writers such as Lancelot Andrewes, Jeremy Taylor, and Thomas Ken re-appropriated from patristic tradition a fuller appreciation of the place of Mary in the prayers of the believer and of the Church. For example, Andrewes in his *Preces Privatae* borrowed from Eastern liturgies when he showed a warmth of Marian devotion "Commemorating the allholy, immaculate, more than blessed mother of God and

evervirgin Mary." This re-appropriation can be traced into the next century, and into the Oxford Movement of the nineteenth century.

47 In the Roman Catholic Church, the continued growth of Marian doctrine and devotion, while moderated by the reforming decrees of the Council of Trent (1545–63), also suffered the distorting influence of Protestant-Catholic polemics. To be Roman Catholic came to be identified by an emphasis on devotion to Mary. The depth and popularity of Marian spirituality in the nineteenth and the first half of the twentieth centuries contributed to the definitions of the dogmas of the Immaculate Conception (1854) and the Assumption (1950). On the other hand, the pervasiveness of this spirituality began to give rise to criticism both within and beyond the Roman Catholic Church and initiated a process of re-reception. This re-reception was evident in the Second Vatican Council which, consonant with the contemporary biblical, patristic, and liturgical renewals, and with concern for ecumenical sensitivities, chose not to draft a separate document on Mary, but to integrate doctrine about her into the Constitution on the Church, *Lumen Gentium* (1964)—more specifically, into its final section

describing the eschatological pilgrimage of the Church (Chapter VIII). The Council intended "to explain carefully both the role of the Blessed Virgin in the mystery of the Word Incarnate and of the Mystical Body, as well as the duties of the redeemed human race towards the God-bearer, mother of Christ and mother of humanity, especially of the faithful" (art. 54). *Lumen Gentium* concludes by calling Mary a sign of hope and comfort for God's pilgrim people (art. 68–69). The Fathers of the Council consciously sought to resist exaggerations by returning to patristic emphases and placing Marian doctrine and devotion in its proper Christological and ecclesial context.

48 Soon after the Council, faced by an unanticipated decline in devotion to Mary, Pope Paul VI published an Apostolic Exhortation, *Marialis Cultus* (1974), to remove doubts about the Council's intentions and to foster appropriate Marian devotion. His review of the place of Mary in the revised Roman rite showed that she has not been 'demoted' by the liturgical renewal, but that devotion to her is properly located within the Christological focus of the Church's public prayer. He reflected on Mary as "a model of the spiritual attitudes with which the Church celebrates

and lives the divine mysteries" (art. 16). She is the model for the whole Church, but also a "teacher of the spiritual life for individual Christians" (art. 21). According to Paul VI, the authentic renewal of Marian devotion must be integrated with the doctrines of God, Christ, and the Church. Devotion to Mary must be in accordance with the Scriptures and the liturgy of the Church; it must be sensitive to the concerns of other Christians and it must affirm the full dignity of women in public and private life. The Pope also issued cautions to those who err either by exaggeration or neglect. Finally, he commended the recitation of the *Angelus* and the Rosary as traditional devotions which are compatible with these norms. In 2002, Pope John Paul II reinforced the Christological focus of the Rosary by proposing five 'mysteries of Light' from the Gospels' account of Christ's public ministry between his Baptism and Passion. "The Rosary," he states, "though clearly Marian in character, is at heart a Christocentric prayer" (*Rosarium Virginis Mariae* 1).

49 Mary has a new prominence in Anglican worship through the liturgical renewals of the twentieth century. In most Anglican prayer books, Mary is again mentioned by name in the Eucharistic prayers.

Further, August 15th has come to be widely celebrated as a principal feast in honour of Mary with Scripture readings, collect, and proper preface. Other feasts associated with Mary have also been renewed, and liturgical resources offered for use on these festivals. Given the definitive role of authorized liturgical texts and practices in Anglican formularies, such developments are highly significant.

50 The above developments show that in recent decades a re-reception of the place of Mary in corporate worship has been taking place across the Anglican Communion. At the same time, in *Lumen Gentium* (Chapter VIII) and the Exhortation *Marialis Cultus* the Roman Catholic Church has attempted to set devotion to Mary within the context of the teaching of Scripture and the ancient common tradition. This constitutes, for the Roman Catholic Church, a re-reception of teaching about Mary. Revision of the calendars and lectionaries used in our Communions, especially the liturgical provision associated with feasts of Mary, gives evidence of a shared process of re-receiving the scriptural testimony to her place in the faith and life of the Church. Growing ecumenical exchange has contributed to the process of re-reception in both Communions.

51 The Scriptures lead us together to praise and bless Mary as the handmaid of the Lord, who was providentially prepared by divine grace to be the mother of our Redeemer. Her unqualified assent to the fulfilment of God's saving plan can be seen as the supreme instance of a believer's 'Amen' in response to the 'Yes' of God. She stands as a model of holiness, obedience, and faith for all Christians. As one who received the Word in her heart and in her body, and brought it forth into the world, Mary belongs in the prophetic tradition. We are agreed in our belief in the Blessed Virgin Mary as *Theotókos*. Our two communions are both heirs to a rich tradition which recognizes Mary as ever virgin, and sees her as the new Eve and as a type of the Church. We join in praying and praising with Mary whom all generations have called blessed, in observing her festivals and according her honour in the communion of the saints, and are agreed that Mary and the saints pray for the whole Church (see below in section D). In all of this, we see Mary as inseparably linked with Christ and the Church. Within this broad consideration of the role of Mary, we now focus on the theology of hope and grace.

C MARY WITHIN THE PATTERN OF GRACE AND HOPE

52 Participation in the glory of God, through the mediation of the Son, in the power of the Spirit is the Gospel hope (cf. 2 Corinthians 3:18; 4:4–6). The Church already enjoys this hope and destiny through the Holy Spirit, who is the 'pledge' of our inheritance in Christ (Ephesians 1:14, 2 Corinthians 5:5). For Paul especially, what it means to be fully human can only be understood rightly when it is viewed in the light of what we are to become in Christ, the 'last Adam', as opposed to what we had become in the old Adam (1 Corinthians 15:42–49, cf. Romans 5:12–21). This eschatological perspective sees Christian life in terms of the vision of the exalted Christ leading believers to cast off sins that entangle (Hebrews 12:1–2) and to participate in his purity and love, made available through his atoning sacrifice (1 John 3:3, 4:10). We thus view the economy of grace from its fulfilment in Christ 'back' into history, rather than 'forward' from its beginning in fallen creation towards the future in Christ. This perspective offers fresh light in which to consider the place of Mary.

53 The hope of the Church is based upon the testimony it has received about the present glory of Christ. The Church proclaims that Christ was not only raised bodily from the tomb, but was exalted to the right hand of the Father, to share in the Father's glory (1 Timothy 3:16, 1 Peter 1:21). Insofar as believers are united with Christ in baptism and share in Christ's sufferings (Romans 6:1–6), they participate through the Spirit in his glory, and are raised up with him in anticipation of the final revelation (cf. Romans 8:17, Ephesians 2:6, Colossians 3:1). It is the destiny of the Church and of its members, the "saints" chosen in Christ "before the foundation of the world", to be "holy and blameless" and to share in the glory of Christ (Ephesians 1:3–5, 5:27). Paul speaks as it were from the future retrospectively, when he says, "those whom God predestined he also called; and those whom he called he also justified; and those whom he justified he also glorified" (Romans 8:30). In the succeeding chapters of Romans, Paul explicates this many-faceted drama of God's election in Christ, keeping in view its end: the inclusion of the Gentiles, so that "all Israel will be saved" (Romans 11:26).

Mary in the Economy of Grace

54 Within this biblical framework we have considered afresh the distinctive place of the Virgin Mary in the economy of grace, as the one who bore Christ, the elect of God. The word of God delivered by Gabriel addresses her as already 'graced', inviting her to respond in faith and freedom to God's call (Luke 1:28, 38, 45). The Spirit is operative within her in the conception of the Saviour, and this "blessed among women" is inspired to sing "all generations will call me blessed" (Luke 1:42, 48). Viewed eschatologically, Mary thus embodies the "elect Israel" of whom Paul speaks—glorified, justified, called, predestined. This is the pattern of grace and hope which we see at work in the life of Mary, who holds a distinctive place in the common destiny of the Church as the one who bore in her own flesh 'the Lord of glory'. Mary is marked out from the beginning as the one chosen, called, and graced by God through the Holy Spirit for the task that lay ahead of her.

55 The Scriptures tell us of barren women who were gifted by God with children—Rachel, Manoah's

wife, Hannah (Genesis 30:1–24, Judges 13, 1 Samuel 1), and those past childbearing—Sarah (Genesis 18:9–15, 21:1–7), and most notably Mary's cousin, Elizabeth (Luke 1:7, 24). These women highlight the singular role of Mary, who was neither barren nor past child-bearing age, but a fruitful virgin: in her womb the Spirit brought about the conception of Jesus. The Scriptures also speak of God's care for all human beings, even before their coming to birth (Psalm 139:13–18), and recount the action of God's grace preceding the specific calling of particular persons, even from their conception (cf. Jeremiah 1:4–5, Luke 1:15, Galatians 1:15). With the early Church, we see in Mary's acceptance of the divine will the fruit of her prior preparation, signified in Gabriel's affirmation of her as 'graced'. We can thus see that God was at work in Mary from her earliest beginnings, preparing her for the unique vocation of bearing in her own flesh the new Adam, in whom all things in heaven and earth hold together (cf. Colossians 1:16–17). Of Mary, both personally and as a representative figure, we can say she is "God's workmanship, created in Christ Jesus for good works which God prepared beforehand" (Ephesians 2:10).

56 Mary, a pure virgin, bore God incarnate in her womb. Her bodily intimacy with her son was all of a piece with her faithful following of him, and her maternal participation in his victorious self-giving (Luke 2:35). All this is clearly testified in Scripture, as we have seen. There is no direct testimony in Scripture concerning the end of Mary's life. However, certain passages give instances of those who follow God's purposes faithfully being drawn into God's presence. Moreover, these passages offer hints or partial analogies that may throw light on the mystery of Mary's entry into glory. For instance, the biblical pattern of anticipated eschatology appears in the account of Stephen, the first martyr (Acts 7:54–60). At the moment of his death, which conforms to that of his Lord, he sees "the glory of God, and Jesus" the "Son of Man" not seated in judgement, but "standing at the right hand of God" to welcome his faithful servant. Similarly, the penitent thief who calls on the crucified Christ is accorded the special promise of being with Christ immediately in Paradise (Luke 23:43). God's faithful servant Elijah is taken up by a whirlwind into heaven (2 Kings 2:11), and of Enoch it is written, "he was attested as having pleased God" as a man of faith, and

was therefore "taken up so that he should not see death; and he was not found because God had taken him" (Hebrews 11:5, cf. Genesis 5:24). Within such a pattern of anticipated eschatology, Mary can also be seen as the faithful disciple fully present with God in Christ. In this way, she is a sign of hope for all humanity.

57 The pattern of hope and grace already foreshadowed in Mary will be fulfilled in the new creation in Christ when all the redeemed will participate in the full glory of the Lord (cf. 2 Corinthians 3:18). Christian experience of communion with God in this present life is a sign and foretaste of divine grace and glory, a hope shared with the whole of creation (Romans 8:18–23). The individual believer and the Church find their consummation in the new Jerusalem, the holy bride of Christ (cf. Revelation 21:2, Ephesians 5:27). When Christians from East and West through the generations have pondered God's work in Mary, they have discerned in faith (cf. *Gift* 29) that it is fitting that the Lord gathered her wholly to himself: in Christ, she is already a new creation in whom "the old has passed away and the new has come" (2 Corinthians 5:17). Viewed from such an eschatological perspective, Mary may be seen

both as a type of the Church, and as a disciple with a special place in the economy of salvation.

The Papal Definitions

58 Thus far we have outlined our common faith concerning the place of Mary in the divine purpose. Roman Catholic Christians, however, are bound to believe the teaching defined by Pope Pius XII in 1950: "that the Immaculate Mother of God, the ever-Virgin Mary, having completed the course of her earthly life, was assumed body and soul into heavenly glory." We note that the dogma does not adopt a particular position as to how Mary's life ended,[10] nor does it use about her the language of death and resurrection, but celebrates the action of

---

10. The reference in the dogma to Mary being assumed 'body and soul' has caused difficulty for some, on historical and philosophical grounds. The dogma leaves open, however, the question as to what the absence of her mortal remains means in historical terms. Likewise, 'assumed body and soul' is not intended to privilege a particular anthropology. More positively, 'assumed body and soul' can be seen to have Christological and ecclesiological implications. Mary as 'God-bearer' is intimately, indeed bodily, related to Christ: his own bodily glorification now embraces hers. And, since Mary bore his body of flesh, she is intimately related to the Church, Christ's body. In brief, the formulation of the dogma responds to theological rather than historical or philosophical questions in relation to Mary.

God in her. Thus, given the understanding we have reached concerning the place of Mary in the economy of hope and grace, we can affirm together the teaching that God has taken the Blessed Virgin Mary in the fullness of her person into his glory as consonant with Scripture and that it can, indeed, only be understood in the light of Scripture. Roman Catholics can recognize that this teaching about Mary is contained in the dogma. While the calling and destiny of all the redeemed is their glorification in Christ, Mary, as *Theotókos*, holds the pre-eminent place within the communion of saints and embodies the destiny of the Church.

59 Roman Catholics are also bound to believe that "the most blessed Virgin Mary was, from the first moment of her conception, by a singular grace and privilege of almighty God and in view of the merits of Christ Jesus the Saviour of the human race, preserved immune from all stain of original sin" (Dogma of the Immaculate Conception of Mary, defined by Pope Pius IX, 1854).[11] The definition teaches that Mary,

---

11. The definition addressed an old controversy about the timing of the sanctification of Mary, in affirming that this took place at the very first moment of her conception.

like all other human beings, has need of Christ as her Saviour and Redeemer (cf. *Lumen Gentium* 53; *Catechism of the Catholic Church* 491). The negative notion of 'sinlessness' runs the risk of obscuring the fullness of Christ's saving work. It is not so much that Mary lacks something which other human beings 'have', namely sin, but that the glorious grace of God filled her life from the beginning.[12] The holiness which is our end in Christ (cf. 1 John 3:2–3) was seen, by unmerited grace, in Mary, who is the proto-type of the hope of grace for humankind as a whole. According to the New Testament, being 'graced' has the connotation of being freed from sin through Christ's blood (Ephesians 1:6–7). The Scriptures point to the efficacy of Christ's atoning sacrifice even for those who preceded him in time (cf. 1 Peter 3:19, John 8:56, 1 Corinthians 10:4). Here again the escha-tological perspective illuminates our understanding of Mary's person and calling. In view of her vocation to

---

12. The assertion of Paul at Romans 3:23—"all have sinned and fall short of the glory of God"—might appear to allow for no exceptions, not even for Mary. However, it is important to note the rhetorical-apologetic context of the general argument of Romans 1–3, which is concerned to show the equal sinfulness of Jews and Gentiles (3:9). Romans 3:23 has a quite specific purpose in context which is unrelated to the issue of the 'sinlessness' or otherwise of Mary.

be the mother of the Holy One (Luke 1:35), we can affirm together that Christ's redeeming work reached 'back' in Mary to the depths of her being, and to her earliest beginnings. This is not contrary to the teaching of Scripture, and can only be understood in the light of Scripture. Roman Catholics can recognize in this what is affirmed by the dogma—namely "preserved from all stain of original sin" and "from the first moment of her conception."

60 We have agreed together that the teaching about Mary in the two definitions of 1854 and 1950, understood within the biblical pattern of the economy of grace and hope outlined here, can be said to be consonant with the teaching of the Scriptures and the ancient common traditions. However, in Roman Catholic understanding as expressed in these two definitions, the proclamation of any teaching as dogma implies that the teaching in question is affirmed to be "revealed by God" and therefore to be believed "firmly and constantly" by all the faithful (i.e. it is *de fide*). The problem which the dogmas may present for Anglicans can be put in terms of Article VI:

> Holy Scripture containeth all things necessary to salvation: so that whatsoever is not read

therein, nor may be proved thereby, is not to be required of any man, that it should be believed as an article of the Faith, or be thought requisite or necessary to salvation.

We agree that nothing can be required to be believed as an article of faith unless it is revealed by God. The question arises for Anglicans, however, as to whether these doctrines concerning Mary are revealed by God in a way which must be held by believers as a matter of faith.

61 The particular circumstances and precise formulations of the 1854 and 1950 definitions have created problems not only for Anglicans but also for other Christians. The formulations of these doctrines and some objections to them are situated within the thought-forms of their time. In particular, the phrases "revealed by God" (1854) and "divinely revealed" (1950) used in the dogmas reflect the theology of revelation that was dominant in the Roman Catholic Church at the time that the definitions were made, and which found authoritative expression in the Constitution *Dei Filius* of the First Vatican Council. They have to be understood today in the light of the way this teaching was refined by the Second Vatican

Council in its Constitution *Dei Verbum*, particularly
in regard to the central role of Scripture in the reception and transmission of revelation. When the
Roman Catholic Church affirms that a truth is
"revealed by God", there is no suggestion of new
revelation. Rather, the definitions are understood to
bear witness to what has been revealed from the
beginning. The Scriptures bear normative witness to
such revelation (cf. *Gift* 19). This revelation is received
by the community of believers and transmitted in
time and place through the Scriptures and through
the preaching, liturgy, spirituality, life, and teaching of
the Church, that draw upon the Scriptures. In *The
Gift of Authority* the Commission sought to explicate
a method by which such authoritative teaching
could arise, the key point being that it needs to be in
conformity with Scripture, which remains a primary
concern for Anglicans and Roman Catholics alike.

62 Anglicans have also questioned whether these doctrines must be held by believers as a matter of faith
in view of the fact that the Bishop of Rome defined
these doctrines "independent of a Council" (cf.
Authority II 30). In response, Roman Catholics have
pointed to the *sensus fidelium*, the liturgical tradition
throughout the local churches, and the active support

of the Roman Catholic bishops (cf. *Gift* 29–30): these were the elements through which these doctrines were recognized as belonging to the faith of the Church, and therefore able to be defined (cf. *Gift* 47). For Roman Catholics, it belongs to the office of the Bishop of Rome that he should be able, under strictly limited conditions, to make such a definition (cf. *Pastor Aeternus* [1870], in *Denzinger-Schönmetzer, Enchiridion Symbolorum* [DS] 3069–3070). The definitions of 1854 and 1950 were not made in response to controversy, but gave voice to the consensus of faith among believers in communion with the Bishop of Rome. They were re-affirmed by the Second Vatican Council. For Anglicans, it would be the consent of an ecumenical council which, teaching according to the Scriptures, most securely demonstrates that the necessary conditions for a teaching to be *de fide* had been met. Where this is the case, as with the definition of the *Theotókos*, both Roman Catholics and Anglicans would agree that the witness of the Church is firmly and constantly to be believed by all the faithful (cf. 1 John 1:1–3).

63 Anglicans have asked whether it would be a condition of the future restoration of full communion that they should be required to accept the definitions of 1854 and 1950. Roman Catholics find it hard to

envisage a restoration of communion in which acceptance of certain doctrines would be requisite for some and not for others. In addressing these issues, we have been mindful that "one consequence of our separation has been a tendency for Anglicans and Roman Catholics alike to exaggerate the importance of the Marian dogmas in themselves at the expense of the other truths more closely related to the foundation of the Christian faith" (*Authority II* 30). Anglicans and Roman Catholics agree that the doctrines of the Assumption and the Immaculate Conception of Mary must be understood in the light of the more central truth of her identity as *Theotókos*, which itself depends on faith in the Incarnation. We recognize that, following the Second Vatican Council and the teaching of recent Popes, the Christological and ecclesiological context for the Church's doctrine concerning Mary is being re-received within the Roman Catholic Church. We now suggest that the adoption of an eschatological perspective may deepen our shared understanding of the place of Mary in the economy of grace, and the tradition of the Church concerning Mary which both our communions receive. Our hope is that the Roman Catholic Church and the Anglican Communion will recognize a common faith in the agreement concerning

Mary which we here offer. Such a re-reception would mean the Marian teaching and devotion within our respective communities, including differences of emphasis, would be seen to be authentic expressions of Christian belief.[13] Any such re-reception would have to take place within the context of a mutual re-reception of an effective teaching authority in the Church, such as that set out in *The Gift of Authority*.

D MARY IN THE LIFE OF THE CHURCH

64 "All the promises of God find their 'Yes' in Christ: that is why we offer the 'Amen' through him, to the glory of God" (2 Corinthians 1:20). God's 'Yes' in Christ takes a distinctive and demanding form as it is

---

13. In such circumstances, the explicit acceptance of the precise wording of the definitions of 1854 and 1950 might not be required of believers who were not in communion with Rome when they were defined. Conversely, Anglicans would have to accept that the definitions are a legitimate expression of Catholic faith, and are to be respected as such, even if these formulations were not employed by them. There are instances in ecumenical agreement in which what one partner has defined as *de fide* can be expressed by another partner in a different way, as for example in the *Common Christological Declaration between the Catholic Church and the Assyrian Church of the East* (1994) or the *Joint Declaration on the Doctrine of Justification between the Roman Catholic Church and the Lutheran World Federation* (1999).

addressed to Mary. The profound mystery of "Christ in you, the hope of glory" (Colossians 1:27) has a unique meaning for her. It enables her to speak the 'Amen' in which, through the Spirit's overshadowing, God's 'Yes' of new creation is inaugurated. As we have seen, this *fiat* of Mary was distinctive, in its openness to God's Word, and in the path to the foot of the cross and beyond on which the Spirit led her. The Scriptures portray Mary as growing in her relationship with Christ: his sharing of her natural family (Luke 2:39) was transcended in her sharing of his eschatological family, those upon whom the Spirit is poured out (Acts 1:14, 2:1–4). Mary's 'Amen' to God's 'Yes' in Christ to her is thus both unique and a model for every disciple and for the life of the Church.

65 One outcome of our study has been awareness of differences in the ways in which the example of Mary living out the grace of God has been appropriated into the devotional lives of our traditions. Whilst both traditions have recognized her special place in the communion of saints, different emphases have marked the way we have experienced her ministry. Anglicans have tended to begin from reflection on the scriptural example of Mary as an inspiration and model for discipleship. Roman Catholics have given

prominence to the ongoing ministry of Mary in the economy of grace and the communion of saints. Mary points people to Christ, commending them to him and helping them to share his life. Neither of these general characterizations do full justice to the richness and diversity of either tradition, and the twentieth century witnessed a particular growth in convergence as many Anglicans were drawn into a more active devotion to Mary, and Roman Catholics discovered afresh the scriptural roots of such devotion. We together agree that in understanding Mary as the fullest human example of the life of grace, we are called to reflect on the lessons of her life recorded in Scripture and to join with her as one indeed not dead, but truly alive in Christ. In doing so we walk together as pilgrims in communion with Mary, Christ's foremost disciple, and all those whose participation in the new creation encourages us to be faithful to our calling (cf. 2 Corinthians 5:17, 19).

66 Aware of the distinctive place of Mary in the history of salvation, Christians have given her a special place in their liturgical and private prayer, praising God for what He has done in and through her. In singing the *Magnificat*, they praise God with her; in the Eucharist, they pray with her as they do with all

God's people, integrating their prayers in the great communion of saints. They recognize Mary's place in "the prayer of all the saints" that is being uttered before the throne of God in the heavenly liturgy (Revelation 8:3–4). All these ways of including Mary in praise and prayer belong to our common heritage, as does our acknowledgement of her unique status as *Theotókos*, which gives her a distinctive place within the communion of saints.

Intercession and Mediation in the Communion of Saints

67 The practice of believers asking Mary to intercede for them with her son grew rapidly following her being declared *Theotókos* at the Council of Ephesus. The most common form today of such intercession is the 'Hail Mary'. This form conflates the greetings of Gabriel and Elizabeth to her (Luke 1:28, 42). It was widely used from the fifth century, without the closing phrase, "pray for us sinners now and at the hour of our death," which was first added in the fifteenth century, and included in the Roman Breviary by Pius V in 1568. The English Reformers criticized this invocation and similar forms of prayer, because they believed that it threatened the unique mediation of

Jesus Christ. Confronted with exaggerated devotion, stemming from excessive exaltation of Mary's role and powers alongside Christ's, they rejected the "Romish doctrine of . . . the Invocation of Saints" as "grounded upon no warranty of Scripture, but rather repugnant to the Word of God" (Article XXII). The Council of Trent affirmed that seeking the saints' assistance to obtain favours from God is "good and useful": such requests are made "through his Son our Lord Jesus Christ, who is our sole redeemer and saviour" (DS 1821). The Second Vatican Council endorsed the continued practice of believers asking Mary to pray for them, emphasising that "Mary's maternal role towards the human race in no way obscures or diminishes the unique mediation of Christ, but rather shows its power . . . in no way does it hinder the direct union of believers with Christ, but rather fosters it" (*Lumen Gentium* 60). Therefore the Roman Catholic Church continues to promote devotion to Mary, while reproving those who either exaggerate or minimize Mary's role (*Marialis Cultus* 31). With this background in mind, we seek a theologically grounded way to draw more closely together in the life of prayer in communion with Christ and his saints.

68 The Scriptures teach that "there is also one mediator between God and humankind, Christ Jesus, himself human, who gave himself as a ransom for all"
(1 Timothy 2:5–6). As noted earlier, on the basis of
this teaching "we reject any interpretation of the role
of Mary which obscures this affirmation" (*Authority
II* 30). It is also true, however, that all ministries of
the Church, especially those of Word and sacrament,
mediate the grace of God through human beings.
These ministries do not compete with the unique
mediation of Christ, but rather serve it and have their
source within it. In particular, the prayer of the
Church does not stand alongside or in place of the
intercession of Christ, but is made through him, our
Advocate and Mediator (cf. Romans 8:34, Hebrews
7:25, 12:24, 1 John 2:1). It finds both its possibility
and practice in and through the Holy Spirit, the
other Advocate sent according to Christ's promise
(cf. John 14:16–17). Hence asking our brothers and
sisters, on earth and in heaven, to pray for us, does
not contest the unique mediatory work of Christ,
but is rather a means by which, in and through the
Spirit, its power may be displayed.

69 In our praying as Christians we address our petitions
to God our heavenly Father, in and through Jesus

Christ, as the Holy Spirit moves and enables us. All such invocation takes place within the communion which is God's being and gift. In the life of prayer we invoke the name of Christ in solidarity with the whole Church, assisted by the prayers of brothers and sisters of every time and place. As ARCIC has expressed it previously, "The believer's pilgrimage of faith is lived out with the mutual support of all the people of God. In Christ all the faithful, both living and departed, are bound together in a communion of prayer" (*Salvation and the Church* 22). In the experience of this communion of prayer, believers are aware of their continued fellowship with their sisters and brothers who have 'fallen asleep', the 'great cloud of witnesses' who surround us as we run the race of faith. For some, this intuition means sensing their friends' presence; for some it may mean pondering the issues of life with those who have gone before them in faith. Such intuitive experience affirms our solidarity in Christ with Christians of every time and place, not least with the woman through whom he became "like us in all things except sin" (Hebrews 4:15).

70 The Scriptures invite Christians to ask their brothers and sisters to pray for them, in and through Christ

(cf. James 5:13–15). Those who are now 'with Christ', untrammelled by sin, share the unceasing prayer and praise which characterizes the life of heaven (e.g. Revelation 5:9–14, 7:9–12, 8:3–4). In the light of these testimonies, many Christians have found that requests for assistance in prayer can rightly and effectively be made to those members of the communion of saints distinguished by their holy living (cf. James 5:16–18). It is in this sense that we affirm that asking the saints to pray for us is not to be excluded as unscriptural, though it is not directly taught by the scriptures to be a required element of life in Christ. Further, we agree that the way such assistance is sought must not obscure believers' direct access to God our heavenly Father, who delights to give good gifts to his children (Matthew 7:11). When, in the Spirit and through Christ, believers address their prayers to God, they are assisted by the prayers of other believers, especially of those who are truly alive in Christ and freed from sin. We note that liturgical forms of prayer are addressed to God: they do not address prayer 'to' the saints, but rather ask them to 'pray for us'. However, in this and other instances, any concept of invocation which blurs the trinitarian economy of grace and hope is to be rejected, as not consonant with Scripture or the ancient common traditions.

The Distinctive Ministry of Mary

71 Among all the saints, Mary takes her place as *Theotókos*: alive in Christ, she abides with the one she bore, still 'highly favoured' in the communion of grace and hope, the exemplar of redeemed humanity, an icon of the Church. Consequently she is believed to exercise a distinctive ministry of assisting others through her active prayer. Many Christians reading the Cana account continue to hear Mary instruct them, "Do whatever he tells you", and are confident that she draws the attention of her son to their needs: "they have no wine" (John 2:1–12). Many experience a sense of empathy and solidarity with Mary, especially at key points when the account of her life echoes theirs, for example the acceptance of vocation, the scandal of her pregnancy, the improvised surroundings of her labour, giving birth, and fleeing as a refugee. Portrayals of Mary standing at the foot of the cross, and the traditional portrayal of her receiving the crucified body of Jesus (the *Pietà*), evoke the particular suffering of a mother at the death of her child. Anglicans and Roman Catholics alike are drawn to the mother of Christ, as a figure of tenderness and compassion.

72 The motherly role of Mary, first affirmed in the Gospel accounts of her relationship to Jesus, has been developed in a variety of ways. Christian believers acknowledge Mary to be the mother of God incarnate. As they ponder our Saviour's dying word to the beloved disciple, "behold your mother" (John 19:27) they may hear an invitation to hold Mary dear as 'mother of the faithful': she will care for them as she cared for her son in his hour of need. Hearing Eve called "the mother of all living" (Genesis 3:20), they may come to see Mary as mother of the new humanity, active in her ministry of pointing all people to Christ, seeking the welfare of all the living. We are agreed that, while caution is needed in the use of such imagery, it is fitting to apply it to Mary, as a way of honouring her distinctive relationship to her son, and the efficacy in her of his redeeming work.

73 Many Christians find that giving devotional expression to their appreciation for this ministry of Mary enriches their worship of God. Authentic popular devotion to Mary, which by its nature displays a wide individual, regional, and cultural diversity, is to be respected. The crowds gathering at some places where Mary is believed to have appeared suggest

that such apparitions are an important part of this devotion and provide spiritual comfort. There is need for careful discernment in assessing the spiritual value of any alleged apparition. This has been emphasized in a recent Roman Catholic commentary.

> Private revelation . . . can be a genuine help in understanding the Gospel and living it better at a particular moment in time; therefore it should not be disregarded. It is a help which is offered, but which one is not obliged to use . . . The criterion for the truth and value of a private revelation is therefore its orientation to Christ himself. When it leads us away from him, when it becomes independent of him or even presents itself as another and better plan of salvation, more important than the Gospel, then it certainly does not come from the Holy Spirit. (Congregation for the Doctrine of the Faith, *Theological Commentary on the Message of Fatima,* 26 June, 2000)

We are agreed that, within the constraints set down in this teaching to ensure that the honour paid to Christ remains pre-eminent, such private devotion is acceptable, though never required of believers.

74 When Mary was first acknowledged as mother of the Lord by Elizabeth, she responded by praising God and proclaiming his justice for the poor in her *Magnificat* (Luke 1:46–55). In Mary's response we can see an attitude of poverty towards God that reflects the divine commitment and preference for the poor. In her powerlessness she is exalted by God's favour. Although the witness of her obedience and acceptance of God's will has sometimes been used to encourage passivity and impose servitude on women, it is rightly seen as a radical commitment to God who has mercy on his servant, lifts up the lowly and brings down the mighty. Issues of justice for women and the empowerment of the oppressed have arisen from daily reflection on Mary's remarkable song. Inspired by her words, communities of women and men in various cultures have committed themselves to work with the poor and the excluded. Only when joy is joined with justice and peace do we rightly share in the economy of hope and grace which Mary proclaims and embodies.

75 Affirming together unambiguously Christ's unique mediation, which bears fruit in the life of the Church, we do not consider the practice of asking Mary and the saints to pray for us as communion

dividing. Since obstacles of the past have been removed by clarification of doctrine, by liturgical reform and practical norms in keeping with it, we believe that there is no continuing theological reason for ecclesial division on these matters.

CONCLUSION

76 Our study, which opens with a careful ecclesial and ecumenical reading of the Scriptures, in the light of the ancient common traditions, has illuminated in a new way the place of Mary in the economy of hope and grace. We together re-affirm the agreements reached previously by ARCIC, in *Authority in the Church II* 30:

- that any interpretation of the role of Mary must not obscure the unique mediation of Christ;

- that any consideration of Mary must be linked with the doctrines of Christ and the Church;

- that we recognize the Blessed Virgin Mary as the *Theotókos*, the mother of God incarnate,

and so observe her festivals and accord her
honour among the saints;

- that Mary was prepared by grace to be
the mother of our Redeemer, by whom
she herself was redeemed and received
into glory;

- that we recognize Mary as a model of holiness, faith, and obedience for all Christians;
and

- that Mary can be seen as a prophetic figure of the Church.

We believe that the present statement significantly
deepens and extends these agreements, setting them
within a comprehensive study of doctrine and devotion associated with Mary.

77 We are convinced that any attempt to come to a rec-
onciled understanding of these matters must begin by
listening to God's word in the Scriptures. Therefore
our common statement commences with a careful
exploration of the rich New Testament witness to

Mary, in the light of overall themes and patterns in the Scriptures as a whole.

- This study has led us to the conclusion that it is impossible to be faithful to Scripture without giving due attention to the person of Mary (paragraphs 6–30).

- In recalling together the ancient common traditions, we have discerned afresh the central importance of the *Theotókos* in the Christological controversies, and the Fathers' use of biblical images to interpret and celebrate Mary's place in the plan of salvation (paragraphs 31–40).

- We have reviewed the growth of devotion to Mary in the medieval centuries, and the theological controversies associated with them. We have seen how some excesses in late medieval devotion, and reactions against them by the Reformers, contributed to the breach of communion between us, following which attitudes toward Mary took divergent paths (paragraphs 41–46).

- We have also noted evidence of subsequent developments in both our Communions, which opened the way for a re-reception of the place of Mary in the faith and life of the Church (paragraphs 47–51).

- This growing convergence has also allowed us to approach in a fresh way the questions about Mary which our two Communions have set before us. In doing so, we have framed our work within the pattern of grace and hope which we discover in Scripture—"predestined . . . called . . . justified . . . glorified" (Romans 8:30) (paragraphs 52–57).

Advances in Agreement

78 As a result of our study, the Commission offers the following agreements, which we believe significantly advance our consensus regarding Mary. We affirm together

- the teaching that God has taken the Blessed Virgin Mary in the fullness of her person into his glory as consonant with

Scripture, and only to be understood in the light of Scripture (paragraph 58);

- that in view of her vocation to be the mother of the Holy One, Christ's redeeming work reached 'back' in Mary to the depths of her being and to her earliest beginnings (paragraph 59);

- that the teaching about Mary in the two definitions of the Assumption and the Immaculate Conception, understood within the biblical pattern of the economy of hope and grace, can be said to be consonant with the teaching of the Scriptures and the ancient common traditions (paragraph 60);

- that this agreement, when accepted by our two Communions, would place the questions about authority which arise from the two definitions of 1854 and 1950 in a new ecumenical context (paragraphs 61–63);

- that Mary has a continuing ministry which serves the ministry of Christ, our unique mediator, that Mary and the saints pray for the whole Church and that the practice of asking Mary and the saints to pray for us is not communion dividing (paragraphs 64–75).

79 We agree that doctrines and devotions which are contrary to Scripture cannot be said to be revealed by God nor to be the teaching of the Church. We agree that doctrine and devotion which focuses on Mary, including claims to 'private revelations', must be moderated by carefully expressed norms which ensure the unique and central place of Jesus Christ in the life of the Church, and that Christ alone, together with the Father and the Holy Spirit, is to be worshipped in the Church.

80 Our statement has sought not to clear away all possible problems, but to deepen our common understanding to the point where remaining diversities of devotional practice may be received as the varied work of the Spirit amongst all the people of God. We believe that the agreement we have here outlined is itself the product of a re-reception by Anglicans and Roman Catholics of doctrine about Mary and that it points to the possibility of further reconciliation, in

which issues concerning doctrine and devotion to Mary need no longer be seen as communion dividing, or an obstacle in a new stage of our growth into visible *koinonia*. This agreed statement is now offered to our respective authorities. It may also in itself prove a valuable study of the teaching of the Scriptures and the ancient common traditions about the Blessed Virgin Mary, the Mother of God incarnate. Our hope is that, as we share in the one Spirit by which Mary was prepared and sanctified for her unique vocation, we may together participate with her and all the saints in the unending praise of God.

MEMBERS OF THE COMMISSION

Anglican Members

The Most Revd Frank Griswold, Presiding Bishop of the Episcopal Church (USA) (*Co-Chair until 2003*)

The Most Revd Peter Carnley, Archbishop of Perth and Primate of the Anglican Church of Australia (*Co-Chair from 2003*)

The Rt Revd John Baycroft, retired Bishop of Ottawa, Canada

Dr E. Rozanne Elder, Professor of History, Western Michigan University, USA

The Revd Professor Jaci Maraschin, Professor of Theology, Ecumenical Institute, Sao Paulo, Brazil

The Revd Dr John Muddiman, University Lecturer in New Testament in the University of Oxford, Mansfield College, Oxford, UK

The Rt Revd Dr Michael Nazir-Ali, Bishop of Rochester, UK

The Revd Canon Dr Nicholas Sagovsky, Canon Theologian of Westminster Abbey, London, UK

The Revd Canon Dr Charles Sherlock, Registrar and Director of Ministry Studies of the Melbourne College of Divinity, Australia

Secretary

The Revd Canon David Hamid, Director of Ecumenical Affairs and Studies, Anglican Communion Office, London, UK (*until 2002*)

The Revd Canon Gregory K. Cameron, Director of Ecumenical Affairs and Studies, Anglican Communion Office, London, UK (*from 2002*)

Archbishop of Canterbury's Observer

The Revd Canon Dr Richard Marsh, Archbishop of Canterbury's Secretary for Ecumenical Affairs, London, UK (*until 1999*)

The Revd Dr Herman Browne, Archbishop of Canterbury's Assistant Secretary for Ecumenical and Anglican Communion Affairs (*from 2000-2001*)

The Revd Canon Jonathan Gough, Archbishop of Canterbury's Secretary for Ecumenism, London, UK (*from 2002*)

Roman Catholic Members

The Rt Revd Cormac Murphy-O'Connor, Bishop of Arundel and Brighton, UK (*Co-Chair until 2000*)

The Most Revd Alexander Brunett, Archbishop of Seattle, USA (*Co-Chair from 2000*)

Sister Sara Butler, MSBT, Professor of Dogmatic Theology, St Joseph's Seminary, Yonkers, New York, USA

The Revd Dr Peter Cross, Lecturer in Systematic Theology, Catholic Theological College, Clayton, Australia

The Revd Dr Adelbert Denaux, Professor, Faculty of Theology, Catholic University, Leuven, Belgium

The Rt Revd Brian Farrell, LC, Secretary, Pontifical Council for Promoting Christian Unity, Vatican City (*from 2003*)

The Rt Revd Walter Kasper, Secretary, Pontifical Council for Promoting Christian Unity, Vatican City (*from 1999-2000*)

The Rt. Revd Malcolm McMahon, OP, Bishop of Nottingham, UK (*from 2001*)

The Revd Professor Charles Morerod, OP, Dean of the Faculty of Philosophy, Pontificia Universita San Tommaso D' Aquino, Rome, Italty (*from 2002*)

The Rt Revd Marc Ouellet, PSS, Secretary, Pontifical Council for Promoting Christian Unity, Vatican City (*from 2001-2002*)

The Revd Jean Tillard, OP, Professor, Dominican Faculty of Theology, Otttawa, Canada (*until 2000, deceased*)

The Revd Professor Liam Walsh, OP, Professor Emeritus, Faculty of Theology, University of Fribourg, Switzerland.

Secretary

The Revd Monsignor Timothy Galligan, Staff member, Pontifical Council for Promoting Christian Unity, Vatican City (*until 2001*)

The Revd Canon Donald Bolen, Staff member, Pontifical Council for Promoting Christian Unity, Vatican City (*from 2001*)

Consultant

Dom Emmanuel Lanne, OSB, Monastery of Chevetogne, Belgium (*from 2000*)

World Council of Churches Observer

The Revd Dr Michael Kinnamon, Dean, Lexington Theological Seminary, Kentucky, USA (*until 2001*)

Administrative Staff

Mrs Christine Codner, Anglican Communion Office, London, UK

Ms Giovanna Ramon, Pontifical Council for Promoting Christian Unity, Vatican City